MW00452011

_To_

_____

From

_____

Date

_____

Grandma,
What Was It Like Growing Up Country?

Artwork by
DONALD ZOLAN

HARVEST HOUSE PUBLISHERS

EUGENE, OREGON

Grandma, What Was It Like Growing Up Country?

Text Copyright © 2009 by Harvest House Publishers
Artwork Copyright © by Donald Zolan

Published by Harvest House Publishers
Eugene, Oregon 97402
www.harvesthousepublishers.com

"You Were a Country Girl" copyright © 2009 by Hope Lyda.

ISBN 978-0-7369-2658-4

Original Oil Paintings by Donald Zolan, © The Zolan Company, LLC. All rights reserved. Artwork is protected by U.S. copyright law and may not be reproduced in whole or in part without written permission. For more information regarding artworks featured in this book, please contact:

> The Zolan Company, LLC
> Attn.: Jennifer Zolan
> e-mail: donaldz798@aol.com
> www.zolan.com

John Deere® is a registered trademark and appears in this book with the permission of Deere and Company, Moline Illinois.

Design and production by Garborg Design Works, Savage, Minnesota

Scripture quotations are taken from the Holy Bible, New Living Translation, copyright ©1996. Used by permission of Tyndale House Publishers, Inc., Wheaton, Illinois 60189, U.S.A. All rights reserved.

Harvest House Publishers has made every effort to trace the ownership of all poems and quotes. In the event of a question arising from the use of a poem or quote, we regret any error made and will be pleased to make the necessary correction in future editions of this book.

All rights reserved. No part of this publication may be reproduced, stored in a retrieval system, or transmitted in any form or by any means—electronic, mechanical, digital, photocopy, recording, or any other—except for brief quotations in printed reviews, without the prior permission of the publishers.

Printed in China

09 10 11 12 13 14 15 / LP / 10 9 8 7 6 5 4 3 2 1

You Were a Country Girl

On the day that you were born, Grandma,
a new life began to unfold.
On the day that you were born,
a new story was about to be told.

I see you as a country girl
Bright-eyed with sun-kissed cheeks,
loving creation's playground
of wheat fields and winding creeks.

Did you help raise chicks or horses,
and pluck apples shiny and red?
Did you turn that ripe fruit into pie,
and bake golden loaves of bread?

Did you float in the sky on a tire swing
and make wishes on stars above?
Did you ever imagine that some day
You'd have a grandchild to love?

Most of all I'd like to know
how you turned out to be
sweet, smart, lovely, and kind
And so very special to me.

On the day that I was born, Grandma,
a new life began to unfold.
On the day that I was born,
your story was ready to be told.

Grandma, please tell me all about what it was like to grow up as a country girl.

Presented to: _____

With love from: _____

Your Story Begins

Grandma, when is your birthday?

_____

Where were you born?

_____

What was going on in the world when you were little? _____

_____

_____

_____

_____

_____

_____

_____

_____

_____

Children are the most wholesome part
of the race, the sweetest, for they are
the freshest from the hand of God.
Whimsical, ingenious, mischievous,
they fill the world with joy and good humor.

HERBERT HOOVER

Do you know how your parents chose your name? _____

_____

_____

_____

_____

_____

_____

_____

_____

_____

_____

_____

*When you were born, you cried and the world rejoiced.
Live your life in such a manner that when you die the
world cries and you rejoice.*

INDIAN PROVERB

Our Family Tree

Grandma, who were your parents? Grandparents? _____
_____
_____

Did you have any brothers or sisters? _____
_____
_____

Describe one of your favorite family memories. _____
_____
_____
_____
_____
_____
_____

What did you enjoy about being a part of your family? _____
_____
_____
_____
_____

In different hours, a man represents each of several of his ancestors, as if there were seven or eight of us rolled up in each man's skin—seven or eight ancestors at least, and they constitute the variety of notes for that new piece of music which his life is.

RALPH WALDO EMERSON

Tell me a family story that was told to you as a girl. _____

_____

_____

_____

_____

_____

_____

_____

_____

_____

_____

_____

_____

Home Sweet Home

Tell me all about your childhood home. _____

_____

_____

_____

_____

What was your room like? _____

_____

_____

_____

Did you have a big yard? _____

_____

_____

Mid pleasures and palaces though we may roam,
Be it ever so humble, there's no place like home;
A charm from the sky seems to hallow us there,
which, seek through the world, is ne'er met with elsewhere.

Home, home, sweet, sweet home!
There's no place like home, oh,
There's no place like home.

JOHN HOWARD PAYNE

8

Describe your first home after you were married. _____
_____
_____
_____
_____
_____
_____

What do you think transforms a house into a home? _____
_____
_____
_____
_____
_____
_____
_____
_____
_____

Starting Your Own Family

Grandma, how did you meet Grandpa? _____

_____

_____

_____

_____

_____

_____

When and where did you get married? _____

_____

What did you like most about your wedding? _____

_____

_____

_____

_____

_____

_____

_____

_____

> Our notion of the perfect society
> embraces the family as its center
> and ornament, and this paradise is
> not secure until children appear to
> animate and complete the picture.
>
> AMOS BRONSON ALCOTT

In time of test, family is best.

PROVERB

What were your deepest joys when you started your own family?

_____

_____

_____

_____

_____

_____

What was my mom/dad like as a child? _____

_____

_____

_____

_____

_____

_____

_____

Traditions and Gatherings

Grandma, what were some of your country childhood traditions? _____

_____

_____

_____

_____

_____

_____

Did you start new traditions when your children were born? _____

_____

_____

_____

_____

_____

_____

What made your family gatherings special? _____

_____

_____

_____

_____

What activities did you enjoy during the holidays? _____

_____

_____

_____

_____

_____

Share with me a tradition you hope I'll pass on to my kids some day. _____

_____

_____

_____

_____

_____

_____

How dear to this heart are the scenes of my childhood,
when fond recollection presents them to view.

SAMUEL WOODWORTH

Memories and Mementos

Do you have any special photos of you or your family? Tell me about them.

_____

_____

_____

_____

What is something   _____

special you have that

belonged to your   _____

mother, father, or   _____

another relative?   _____

_____

_____

_____

What memories of your parents, children, and life do you want to share with me?

_____

_____

_____

_____

If you could share a "snapshot" of a special time
or place in your life, what would that image be of?

_____

_____

_____

_____

_____

_____

_____

When you picture my future, Grandma, what do you hope it looks like?

_____

_____

What greater thing is there for _____

human souls than to feel that _____

they are joined for life—to _____

be with each other in silent _____

unspeakable memories. _____

GEORGE ELIOT

COUNTRY LIFE... *Childhood*

Play Time

When you had free time, what was the first thing you liked to do? _____

_____

_____

_____

_____

_____

Did you have a favorite book? Favorite movie? Toy? _____

_____

_____

_____

_____

_____

_____

_____

One of my earliest recollections is of playing with books in my father's study, building houses and bridges of the big dictionaries and diaries, looking at pictures, pretending to read, and scribbling on blank pages whenever pen or pencil could be found.

LOUISA MAY ALCOTT

What was your favorite outdoor activity? _____

_____

_____

_____

_____

_____

What game would you love to play with me? _____

_____

_____

_____

_____

*A garden of God is our childhood, each day
a festival with laughter and play.*

MICAH J. LEBENSOHN

At the Kitchen Table

Describe what your family mealtime was like as a child. _____

_____

_____

_____

_____

What was your favorite meal for breakfast? lunch? dinner? _____

_____

_____

_____

What was your least favorite food? _____

_____

_____

Did you have a favorite mealtime prayer or topic of conversation? _____

_____

_____

_____

One can say everything best over a meal.
GEORGE ELIOT

What is the most important ingredient
to make family meal times special?

_____

_____

_____

_____

_____

An honest laborious Country-man,
with good Bread, Salt, and a little
Parsley, will make a contented
Meal with a roasted Onion.

JOHN EVELYN

Share with me some of your favorite recipes. _____

_____

_____

_____

_____

_____

_____

_____

_____

Country School

What was school like when you were a student? _____

_____

_____

_____

_____

_____

_____

Which schools did you go to? _____

_____

_____

_____

How did a teacher or a school experience influence your life? _____

_____

_____

_____

_____

_____

_____

A grandmother is a little bit parent, a little bit teacher, and a little bit best friend.

AUTHOR UNKNOWN

What was your favorite subject? _____

_____

What kind of activities were you involved in throughout your school years? _____

_____

You do not really understand something unless you can explain it to your grandmother.

PROVERB

_____

_____

_____

_____

_____

_____

_____

_____

_____

_____

Helping Hands

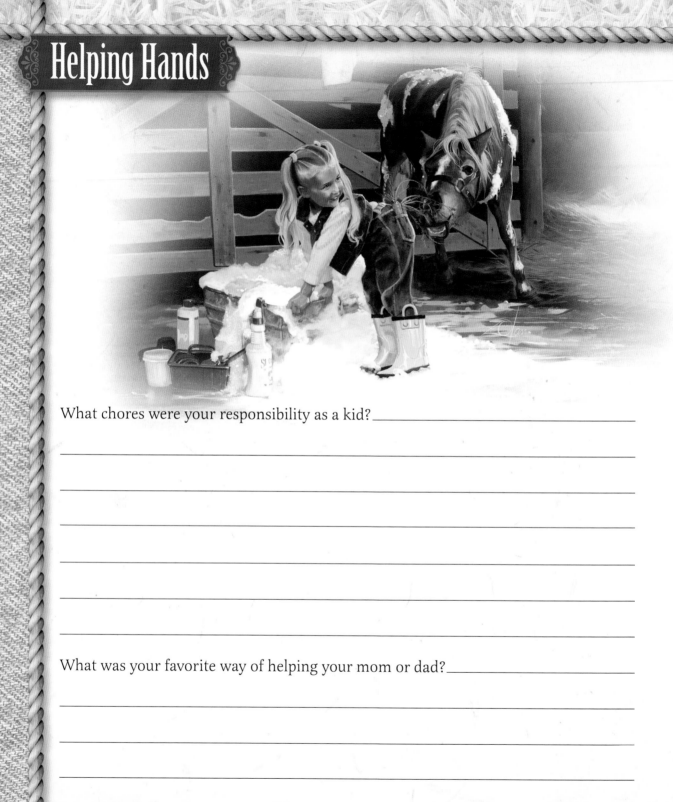

What chores were your responsibility as a kid? _____

_____

_____

_____

_____

_____

_____

What was your favorite way of helping your mom or dad? _____

_____

_____

_____

How did the country life teach you to help one another? _____

_____

_____

_____

_____

_____

_____

_____

What should I know about being a good helper?

If you've got a job to do,
    Do it now!
If it's one you wish were through
    Do it now!
If you're sure the job's your own,
Don't hem and haw and groan—
    Do it now!
Don't put off a bit of work,
    Do it now!
It doesn't pay to shirk,
    Do it now!

ANONYMOUS

23

Farm Friends

Grandma, what pets did you have as a child? What were their names?

_____

_____

_____

_____

_____

_____

_____

_____

Did you grow up around other farm animals?

_____

_____

_____

_____

_____

_____

_____

I like pigs. Dogs look up to us. Cats look down on us. Pigs treat us as equals.

WINSTON CHURCHILL

Which animals do you love the most? _____

_____

_____

_____

What is your favorite story about a furry friend? _____

_____

_____

_____

_____

_____

_____

_____

_____

_____

_____

_____

Our perfect companions never have fewer than four feet.
COLETTE

Creation's Wonder

What kind of garden did your family have when you grew up in the country? _____

_____

_____

_____

_____

List the types of trees, plants, and flowers that grew around your childhood home.

_____

_____

_____

_____

_____

_____

_____

_____

Grandchildren are the crowning glory of the aged;
parents are the pride of their children.

THE BOOK OF PROVERBS

How did you enjoy nature? Did you climb trees, play hide-
and-seek among the corn stalks, or listen to the frogs at night?

_____

_____

_____

_____

_____

_____

I love to think of nature as an unlimited
broadcasting station, through which God
speaks to us every hour, if we will only tune in.

GEORGE WASHINGTON CARVER

_____

If you could show me a special outdoor place from your childhood, what would it be?

_____

_____

_____

_____

Why was it so meaningful to you? _____

_____

_____

_____

Best of Friends

Who were your friends when you were growing up? _____

_____

_____

_____

_____

_____

What were your favorite activities to do with friends? _____

_____

_____

_____

_____

_____

_____

*Let us be grateful to people who make
us happy. They are the charming
gardeners who make our souls blossom.*
MARCEL PROUST

How were you a good friend? _____

_____

_____

_____

_____

_____

_____

Soul mates are people who bring out the best in you. They are not perfect but are always perfect for you.

AUTHOR UNKNOWN

Grandma, share a story about one of your special times with friends. _____

_____

_____

_____

_____

_____

_____

_____

_____

_____

_____

Country Courage

What were some of the hard times your family experienced? _____

_____

_____

_____

_____

_____

_____

_____

_____

How did you and your family handle the tough days? _____

_____

_____

_____

_____

_____

_____

Where does your courage come from, Grandma?_____

_____

_____

_____

_____

_____

What advice do you have for me when I am afraid or uncertain?_____

_____

_____

_____

_____

_____

We can easily manage if we will only
take, each day, the burden appointed to
it. But the load will be too heavy for us if
we carry yesterday's burden over again
today, and then add the burden of the
morrow before we are required to bear it.

JOHN NEWTON

Country Faith

Did your family go to church when you were a girl? _____

_____

_____

_____

_____

_____

What was your favorite prayer for bedtime and mealtime? _____

_____

_____

_____

_____

_____

_____

Faith in a prayer-hearing God will make a prayer-loving Christian.
ANDREW MURRAY

Trust in the Lord with all your heart; do not depend on your own understanding. Seek his will in all you do, and he will show you which path to take.

THE BOOK OF PROVERBS

What is your most treasured verse or memory from church? _____

_____

_____

_____

_____

_____

Grandma, what is your prayer for me?

_____

_____

_____

_____

_____

_____

_____

_____

_____

Good Times

What or who made you laugh as a child? _____

_____

_____

_____

_____

_____

_____

Do you remember a joke or funny song from your childhood? _____

_____

_____

Tell me about a time when you were really happy. _____

_____

_____

_____

_____

_____

_____

_____

_____

_____

The happiest moments
of my life have been
the few which I have
passed at home in the
bosom of my family.

THOMAS JEFFERSON

Share with me a story from your life that still makes you laugh. _____

_____

_____

_____

_____

_____

_____

_____

_____

Wishin' and A-Hopin'

Grandma, what did you daydream about as a girl? _____

_____

_____

_____

_____

What did you want to be when you grew up? _____

_____

_____

When you said your bedtime prayers, who and what did you pray for? _____

_____

_____

_____

_____

_____

_____

_____

_____

Every wish is like a prayer—with God.
ELIZABETH BARRETT BROWNING

Today, what are the dreams you have for your life? _____

_____

_____

_____

_____

_____

What are your wishes for me, Grandma?

_____

_____

_____

_____

_____

_____

_____

_____

_____

Do not pray for gold and jade and
precious things; pray that your children
and grandchildren may all be good.

CHINESE PROVERB

Beauty to Behold

What was the most beautiful view you've ever seen? _____

_____

_____

_____

_____

_____

_____

How did you express your creativity
when you were young?

_____

_____

_____

_____

_____

_____

_____

_____

What colors, music, art, or poetry inspire you? _____

_____

_____

_____

_____

_____

What made you feel beautiful as a girl? _____

_____

_____

_____

_____

What beauty do you hope is a part of my life? _____

_____

_____

_____

_____

Everybody needs beauty as well as bread, places to play in and pray in, where nature may heal and give strength to body and soul.

JOHN MUIR

Being Neighborly

What was the town or community like that you grew up in? _____

_____

_____

_____

_____

_____

_____

_____

_____

_____

Did you participate in your town's celebrations, parades, or the county fair? _____

_____

_____

_____

_____

_____

_____

> While the spirit of neighborliness was important on the frontier because neighbors were so few, it is even more important now because our neighbors are so many.
>
> LADY BIRD JOHNSON

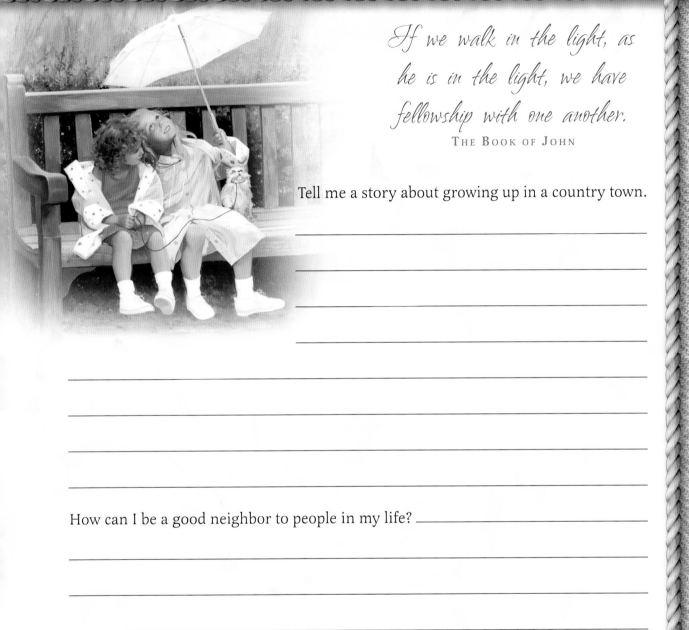

If we walk in the light, as he is in the light, we have fellowship with one another.

THE BOOK OF JOHN

Tell me a story about growing up in a country town.

_____

_____

_____

_____

_____

_____

_____

_____

How can I be a good neighbor to people in my life? _____

_____

_____

_____

_____

_____

_____

Joys of Grandparenting

Grandma, where were you when you found out that my story had begun?

_____

_____

_____

_____

Describe one of the most surprising joys of being a grandparent. _____

_____

_____

_____

_____

What do you love most about being a grandma? _____

_____

_____

_____

_____

What do you want me to know about you?

_____

_____

_____

_____

_____

_____

_____

_____

_____

_____

_____

_____

_____

You might say that the grandmother falls all over herself to try to show her appreciation for her grandchild. It goes right back to those wishes that were made for them when they were little girls: the wish that they would live to become grandmothers someday.

HENRY OLD COYOTE

The Harvest of Country Life

How was country living different then compared to life now? _____

_____

_____

_____

_____

_____

_____

What is the most important lesson you
learned from growing up country?

_____

_____

_____

_____

_____

_____

_____

The best things in life are nearest: Breath in your nostrils, light in your eyes, flowers at your feet, duties at your hand, the path of right just before you. Then do not grasp at the stars, but do life's plain, common work as it comes, certain that daily duties and daily bread are the sweetest things in life.

ROBERT LOUIS STEVENSON

Tell me all about your favorite aspects of country living. _____

_____

_____

_____

_____

_____

What do you hope I experience that was a part of your childhood?_____

_____

_____

_____

_____

A Letter from Grandma

_____

_____

_____

_____

_____

_____

_____

_____

_____

_____

_____

_____

Grandma, what would you want me to know most of all? _____

_____

_____

_____

_____

_____

_____

_____

_____

_____

_____

_____

_____

_____

_____

I share these memories with my grandchild,

_____

With love,

_____

Family life is full of major and minor crises—the ups and downs of health, success and failure in career, marriage, and divorce—and all kinds of characters. It is tied to places and events and histories. With all of these felt details, life etches itself into memory and personality. It's difficult to imagine anything more nourishing to the soul.

THOMAS MOORE